MY BROTHER AND I

By Ayesha Rodriguez

This book is dedicated to my brother.
I love you and I am so proud of you!

Copyright © 2020 by Ayesha Rodriguez

All rights reserved. No part of this publication may be reproduced or transmitted in any form or means electronic or mechanical, including photocopy, recording, or any information storage, and retrieval system without the permission of both publisher and author, except in the case of brief excerpts used in critical articles and reviews. Unauthorized reproduction of any part of this work is illegal and is punishable by law.

Library of Congress Cataloging-in-Publication Data
ISBN: 978-1-7356650-4-7

Publisher Jaye Squared Youth Empowerment Services, INC.
Website: www.ayesharodriguez.com

Illustration copyright © 2020 by Rina Risnawati

Layout Design by Susan Gulash
Gulash Graphics, Lutz, FL

My brother and I are like a hand and glove.

He is one of the people that I truly love.

We go outside. We like to race and play ball.

I am always there to pick him up if he falls.

We play with our toys and mess up the place.

We pretend we are superheroes and put on our capes!

We clean up our room and do our chores.

We work together quickly because they are such a bore!

We practice what we learn so we can do well in school.

We like getting good grades. It's really cool!

We read lots of books and play with our bricks.

We pretend to do magic and perform great tricks!

Sometimes we watch movies or play video games.

It's fun being together!
Without him, it's not the same.

There are plenty of times that he gets me in trouble.

But when I need his help,
he is there on the double!

Through the ups and downs,
the smiles and the frowns...

I am so glad that my brother is around.

My brother forever, my friend he will always be.
Our bond can never be broken.
I am happy we are family.

Discussion Questions

1. What do you love most about your brother?

2. Having someone to play with can be so much fun. What are your favorite things to do together?

3. Sometimes siblings do not get along. What is something that gets you upset?

The word **compromise** means to give up a little bit of what you want so that everyone can agree.

4. What are ways that you can compromise when you two have a problem?

5. It is good to practice kindness. Name a few kind things that you can do for your brother.

6. It is very important that family takes care of each other. If your brother is sick or sad, how can you help her feel better?

7. Teamwork makes the dream work. Can you think of ways that you can work together to clean up faster?

8. Imagine that you and your brother are superheroes.

What would your names be? What would be your super powers? What would your costumes look like? How would you help save the world?

About the Author

Ayesha Rodriguez is an author, speaker, educator and entrepreneur. Most importantly, she is the mom to two wonderful children. She is dedicated to creating books and products that positively reflect the diversity of children. She enjoys spending quality time with loved ones and traveling.

To learn more about her, please visit: www.ayesharodriguez.com

www.ingramcontent.com/pod-product-compliance
Lightning Source LLC
Chambersburg PA
CBHW051306110526
44589CB00025B/2959